This Messy Entertainment book belongs to:

....

....

Published By Messy Entertainment Ltd 2017
ISBN 978-1-9998015-3-3
Messy Entertainment Ltd
www.messyentertainment.com

The Shallows Of The Sea - Manatee 2017 © Messy Entertainment Ltd
All rights reserved.

This book or any portion thereof may not be reproduced or used
in any manner whatsoever without the express written permission
of the publisher except for the use of brief quotations in a book review.

I suck in lots of air
that fills up my chest,
then I dive again
but I have to hold my breathe.

If all the places are too cold and we start to feel frustration, we swim towards the warmer waters by the power stations.

ALL ABOUT ME...

Manatee

- We eat mostly seaweeds and vegetation
- We can live for an average of 30 years in the wild
- We are pretty fast we can swim up to 20 mph
- Adult manatees can grow to be 10 feet long
- We need to eat 7-15% of our bodyweight each day

We live in the Atlantic Ocean, near to the equator

Conservation Status

- Critically Endangered
- Endangered
- *Vulnerable*
- Near Threatened
- Least Concerned

Manatees are considered to be vulnerable although numbers in Florida are increasing in 2017.

Manatee

Match the pairs to find the odd one out?

Can you find the way through the maze?

Can you find 7 differences?

Can you add together these boats?

🚤🚤 + 🚤🚤🚤🚤 = ☐

2 + 🚤 = ☐

🚤🚤🚤 + ☐ = 5

🚤🚤 + ☐ = 8

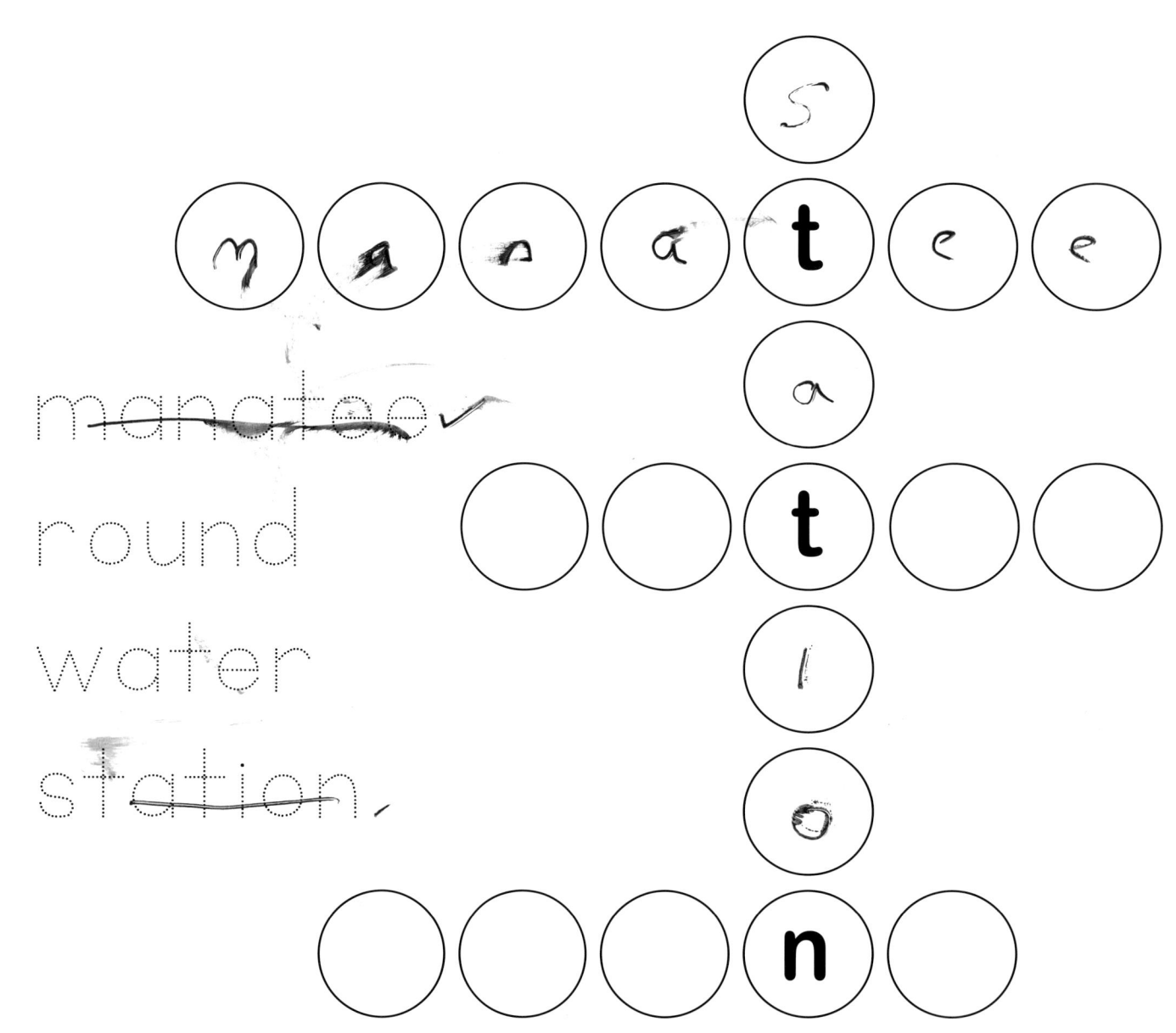

How many manatees can you count?

Can you find these words?

| MANATEE | MAMMAL | WATER | SEAWEED |
| OCEAN | SWIM | ROUND | FRIENDS |

```
D F R I E N D S
W F M A M M A L
A H A Q W I X S
T R N M T W Q E
E H A B K S U A
R U T A L P H W
O C E A N I G E
A S E T U O F E
U D I R O U N D
```

Can you fill in the missing words?

Seaweed is my favourite ……………………………………

I like to …………………………………… in shallow waters.

I hold my …………………………………… when I dive.

I have really thick ……………………… to keep me warm.

swim   food   skin   breath

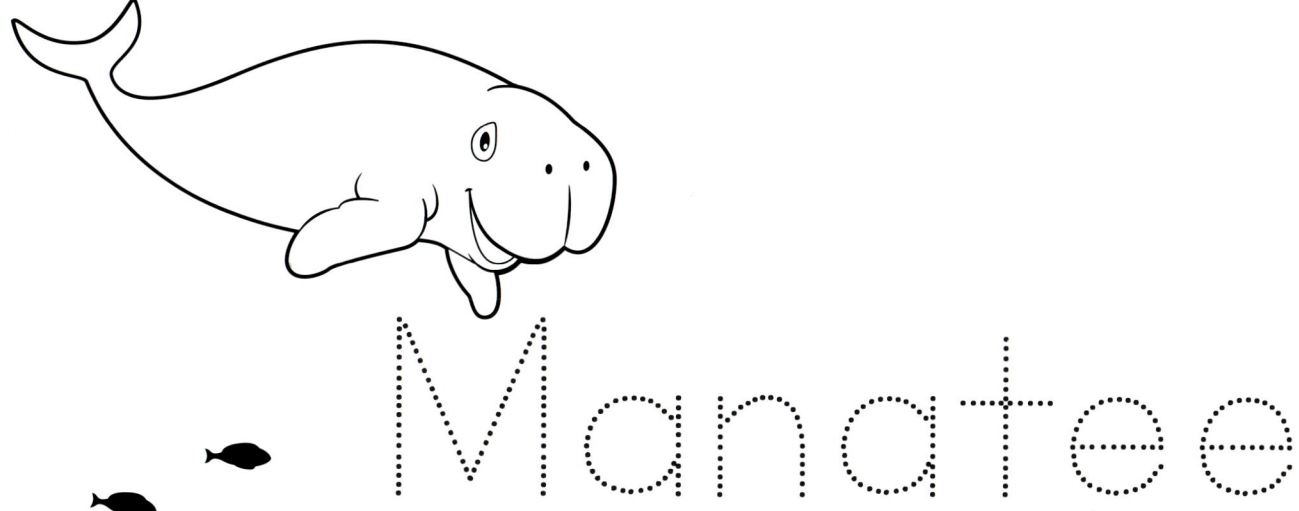

Manatee

Can you complete this picture by connecting the dots?

www.messyentertainment.com

Search 'Messy Entertainment'
for books, apps & much more.